Characters of Age

Corrigan James Moran

Toad Press
San Antonio

ISBN-13: 978-0615914398
ISBN-10: 061591439X

Author Photo by Caitlin Moran

First Edition

KRAMA

MADYA

NGOKO

KRAMANTARA

Atlas *125*

FOR RAYCHEL AMY CHIN
March 18, 1996 – April 2, 2014

Characters of Age

KRAMA

"I will walk through your speech
breathing in the fever and age
you mean to make on me."

-JOHN PHILLIP SANTOS
"From the Brown Book"

Tasseomancy

I was born boiling.
I have become diluted
colder over years.

People, books, ideas,
      every taste I've held
      every friend I've lost
      every love swallowed whole
      every voice I've heard
      every word written
are loose leaves
of different teas,
and I am steeping.

I am pulling my depth,
deepening in the flavor
of everything
I am becoming.
Philosophers call this tabula rasa,
psychologists, neuroplasticity.

The longer I steep,
entropy chews me from heat.
These leaves have leached.

I have poured myself
into so much.
I am losing more
than my clarity,
Trust that this
is only taste.

I am growing bitter.
I am becoming
too cold. Please,
take a sip.

Globes

I am mapping only the countries
throughout my hunger
unable to remember
themselves, those pulling
down their heated hammers
for an echo,

calling to the grand
accordion some
slinkied notice.

All that leads
to me now is all that
is doored into old months.

My hunger is unlocking,
opening each door
to remember
she was a woman who tripped
over an hourglass, and
kicked it afterwards
in an angry nothing.

This girl who kicks over
hourglasses, this inverted
bottle of lust, flip of
a switch,
wineglass full of sun,
horizon stumbling out of night.

Pillars

They walk away, close
together a moved Gomorrah,
and if I turn around,
pillar of salt.

I sit stringing
letters together clay
from smoke, burns each
finger down this
pillar of ash.

I oil looms stuck, tangled
in the webs of Moirai. Deadened
hairs strand that libraried
drip, weaving only
the split or death.

I made plans for this
Friday, mapping my calendar a
pillar of ambition.

And next Thursday, dilemma
turns loneliness into a question
or answers easy seclusion.
To think,
there is music stuck somewhere
that I can't put to tongue. So
kept down as harsh and dwindling
as beer as butterfly in my gut.

And all I have
to show for what

I have left unsaid,
to show for every time
I have turned around,
is just a
pillar of words.

Children's Crusade

A lie,
short and sweet
in the taste of opium,

picking
spiderwebs from my hair,

react.

Lysergic Myopia

I found her first.
This girl a glass of ice
water splintered through my hands,
my wineglass hands.

And with this burdened
ambition the holes boring
through my idea of her allow
coming in at a distance.
Pouring the ice water, acid
haired, her earth-eyed opposition,

wormwood eye,
shallow water eye.

Crescent moon-frowned,
lunar grinned, a mouth
full of white sails
full of blind wind.

The rest of you,
of her so full of holes,
porous chambers,
chosen ventricle.
I've lost count of our distance.

I've memorized the
sound of bottles laughing
against one another
in a close room,

that glassy tumbling
into her acidity has
stringed me here
in this binge of language
I can no longer.

Tides

I want to feel the way
that words describe feeling,
laced through books
in an embered mimic,

yet some numbed pathos
of childhood and peopled
chains hold me close to a
solid cynicism capable
first of incapability.

My every step towards acceptance
is a wet footprint from humanity,
holding back as hard as tide,
only to return beneath night,
the crushed ambition of sand
caking horizon's knees,

to recede as before
back into the ocean,
waiting.

Silvering

Lend me the
mirrors of your madness,
the convenient size
of your heart
to your fist.

This death
stare being only
a staircase, my eyes
into your eyes
climbing a fist
fight into chest.

Do not roll
up that window.
These door locks
are not deaf.

Your luck sleeps
in fountains, pockets
away empty until you
flip and pick a side.

Heads or tails,
mirror or memory.

Inside Voices

The legs cross in song.
Language has reclined
for a blood transfusion.

There is a war being waged
in our ancestry.
Casualties frail page numbers.

Your dog tag is a bookmark.

Not a soul has died in our time
lines, but the bloodbirth of
song inks our skin into holy ground.

The gravemeats are warmed
under our tombstone made microphone.
We share the epitaph
like a pot of tea.

I will clap for your every word,
twice for those I do not know.

I will fall in your every war,
twice for those I understand.

Schadenfreude

Our ancestors spend their
      sunrises and moonfalls
    pouring sand down staircases
         in attempt to lighten
     the futility of written word
and the very description of madness.

Breathing Treatment

I inhale
my mother.
The lung-sprouts thick
wet roots melancholy
splitting out of
every staircase,
forming promises into
platitudes. Gospel of
faded receipts.

The days were felt
        sharp as burn,
        vague as taste.

This contrasts the
warm downed
 tongue brush
    stroke of
      white wine
  to the
    cold feeling of pills
on the tongue,
dreaming guts.

My life you sipped
through fingertips
        tasting curled metals and
        dirt clenched teething to
a trigger spoken in
inward warning.

Each regret felt
pierced maternal,
wetlimp on a fishhook,
soggy from riverbank backwash.
They hardly cry hardly,
leave themselves alone.

The nothing but solitude
in a enclave glued together
the pulled marks of faces
painted in dream wrinkles,
nightmare's skinny ambition.

All the while,
grief twists silent in words
making use as new nails.

A bond between burns
fills the bridge's emptiness.
In the blood beneath
a careful breath,
I exhale
my father.

Altamonte
or Where the Mother Waits

There are bricks in braincorner
holding down the pages.
Memory boils to a paperwait.

My lips are curler.
My favorite dream
is a swimming pool.
Everything else
is consequence, chlorine
keep your eyes open under
water as long as you can,

the wall folds in corner
around us like a mantra.
The ceiling remains a ceiling.

Everything, she says,
sleep it off.

Cage Symmetry

I live within walls.
Not every asylum
holds madness, even admits.

The tiles on this
ground are a chessboard
for pieces unable
of certain trajectory

Each accusing the others
of being pawns
and bishops
and kings.

And I sleep amongst them,
uncertain remaining unspoken,
written although unclear.

All constructs are required
to have clearly marked exits.

Architects have
to design a way out.
But step into the out.

Over and over, nothing ever
really ends.

Depth

Half shivering translucence
anchors my age
into yours

blood or bone or dust
deep.

I paint age over
our curvatures
and feign a tipping
surprise.

I used to love
the way my skin
fell across holding
yours, and now
the hold's only
as loose as the
half-born stars we
splashed against the
walls of your room.

Our astrology lies
blind with blanket,
the dust of us anchors
our eyes as lilies
in this rain. How
could we have known
our roots were deep
enough for us to drown?

Noblesse Oblige

Your inhabited
density grasped by limbs,
(contrast to the branches above)
withered roots writhe deep
in your fertile skin.
Hold tightly - hugging lovely
in complete.

Nostalgia squeezed during
windswept days.
Rain organized your face.
The tree stands unmoving.

After the tree has grown
enough towards your burning
surrogate womb and roots lie
in blood-reach congealed
towards Tartarus you will both die.

Beginning to wither,
branches soon take the
fingernail roots as teeth
sinking in the meatwrinkled sky.

And those comforting
winds that once tested
your bond, now they leave
you fears only left in bookshelves.
For you know near the breeze
shall tear out

the lifeless husk,
ripping familiarity from
your earth.
You cannot let it
happen without you.

But as it does,
(leaving only a crater)
a desolate body will lay
upon your breast,

emaciated roots-

                        reaching
                        their
                        hands from
                        both sides.

                Decay cleans you
        like a garden hose.
                On the stairs in
        the dirt, I will wait
                with glasses full
        of ice.

                You'll feel
        hollowed.
Rain coaxes soil to emptiness.

Filled again, waiting
for another sprout.
Once ambitiously empty,
now just full and wet.

Placebo

This kind of false
compassion, lending
shoulder like the first
door in a room:

promise minus
punctuation at the end

oceans eating shores
mountains not to laugh
their boundless mouthful ends,
their geognostic mumbles.

With such earth,
I weigh that there
are bloodstains in my empathy.
Iron ponders it down
like an anchor,

pulling it further
and further
into the seas of what we hide in
between our selves like continents,
oceans where our ironies become
animals with hungered geography.

Shores grin sands from dead
coral. A reef hugged around
this island we never
visited. Ruin waved
age's always
gnashing shells.

And I've been told that all
of those who anchor in the
dead are more than men.

Nets

Human snow globes
hang their circles
around your neck.
The shape of being
cursed in the birth
mark of your blessings.

In the center eternal
our apple-cored unchange.

Shaken the beauty busts
from our feet. Lusts in color
to dangle at age's sanded haste.

Every snow globe
is an hourglass.
I have lost the will to count.

Age is a measure of
movement. Your beauty
is a gauge of center-
its own broken compass.

What I am doing
can be the opposite
of circling. Knowing
this, I ask you to never
let me settle completely.

Knowledge of Good and Evil

At a place I once lived,
there was a plant
vining over one of the
benches.

Between leaves let out heart
dense fruit. They were once
green, but smoked to
red in too much sun.

They fell in October
on the ground, on the other
bench. They fell in red.
And I found their
meaning some time
later, the same month.

I showed them to
one other person.
I stepped on one in
front of her.

And the pop was hollow,
eggs full of nothing.

Hunger

I want to domino plunge my
wakes with you,
a string of dusty motels.

I want to count
sounds of sun
light plucking from
curtain flecks in air.

Above our bed, we'll
roll and crumble out
of dream. I'll peel the
crescents of old moon
from your hair.

Together we'll look
at each other and speak
of our hunger as if we didn't
already know what we wanted
when we woke.

Opposite of a Wound

How can I introduce you
without making you
into something else?

I've warmed my hands
in your pupiled coal
singing seeds
untangling flame.

There's some poetry that
won't squeeze into words.
Such as your laugh like
boys breaking cascarones.
I can't shackle with sentence
how you scribed some foreign
tongue off an old lamp.

You could tell me you hold liquor
like a suitcase and I would still
want to hold you like a violin.
And I cannot play the violin.

Because nowadays, these feelings
are tourists, folding maps
to a country that can only be folded.
I've charted half of this
hunger in a jar of raisins.

The way your eyes take to no pole,
folding my direction in fourths,
just to tell me to stop talking
because the waitress is coming
back for the third time.

But there's a poem in how
you can capture a cat
on your eyelid and call me
conscious in the same
minute and a half,

a rope in your skin
pulling the crunched socks
of autumn leaves the pieces
of fall following. A way
your hair is frayed light
in library's carpet dripping
no particular language.

My hand goes for yours like a pen,
and now I cannot think of anything
else to write.

Your goodbye's now a voice
mail I have memorized. I can
not forget the taste
of each envelope I could never send.

You have extinguished
ice with the strength
of daffodil and napalm.
Pushed indifference
too
far
down a needleplunger of geoglossum
petals.

Wrapped what is in
complete
with greasy handprints of children
on the windows
on all of the windows,
and I have swallowed
transparency whole,
a lockbox with too many keys.

But I could swear
there are curtains
to your fingertips
and there is a grace
in how you dodge
bicycles and never
judge half cups of coffee.

There is a way you have
timed unlit cigarettes
like footsteps and love
like the soft hum of a microwave.

You asked for this
for happiness,
but you said
It is way too early
in the morning to get lost.

MADYA

"The age demanded that we sing
And cut away our tongue."

-ERNEST HEMINGWAY
"The Age Demanded"

Monday

I light the intro burn
 and watch the day set
 through my garage.

Winds carry the smoke
 that once filtered
 my guts from reason,
 carving neither of
 our names into trees.

She reverses her car further
 and further in
 to the street,
 finding herself
 the common ambivalence
 of each day.

Upon the fulcrum's sternum,
 a balance begins between
 consistency and spontaneity.
 It goes.
She turns and drives to work.

Leaving today lit
 I scrub oils full
 of drowned shamans,
 rubbed forgotten the first
 burns of summer's warmth.

In the holes of our memory
celebration is poured in surges.

We desecrate the wines of our old
  creator. Books of remembrance
  lose importance and wrap
  cigarettes to toast to endings.

Our wine seeps through this evening,
  tomorrow caught in coffee
  filter mouth.
Yesterday holds together another burn.

The day burnt
  through my garage.
And my mouth hangs, like
  memory, from her cigarette.

Egg

I was hollowed for your hands.
My life yolked,
poured thick from me.
Heavy emptying.

Filled again
I am your cascarone.
Break me
into your hair.

Let pieces stay
for days tangled
in color.

Let my shell fall
into bedsheets, stick
in the shower drain.
Let me cut the soft
spots of your feet.

Pretend I am pain
full with every step.

Cold Blankets

As we shared winter's
warm belly in
between us
we knew before we felt,

the other piercing
spine's trunk through and
through with sewing antlers,
sowing fungal spores.

And I said to you,
(in our air
 shared a
   last smoke)
There is more to read
than words on this earth.

And with ease
closed a human being
as one closes an envelope.

Emulsion

The evaporating person
reacts into the squeeze
of meaning
as if echoes compounded
from familiar
thought to familiar experience
raggedly
forming
comfort.

Yet when such stimulus
roots hard into feeling
wrings loose the blood
of stability,
the necessity of loss
condenses, becomes action.

Experiencing
embodying an absence,
working this convenience as an end,
the lack of a person's
presence a means
of empty furthering space.

The evaporating person will always
lead to the engulfing
of something
that once was
as in flame,
as in uterus.

All at once
etches her entirety
into the art of
memory alone.

Front Lawns

She frowns at the telephone
as if to make it silent.

Each of the numbers
fold a lettered four,
prompting her in brief
to map these feelings by
order of relevance.

The beginning of anything, she says,
is nothing but a hungry phone call.
The quick punch of hairs under
nails, holding her palm in my hand.

Her voice is so harsh
on the other line, scratching
into the screens, windows bottled
breathing.
She wonders how one goes
about lightening a silence.

Her wordlessness wakes
on someone else's nightstand.

Some calls she finds her
self jammed into a story
webbed with front lawns
and gigantic holidays, grass
naturing her sour groove
into honey, her futility stretching

across a nation of
maps in telephone lines,
but at every end, only one
will notice how loud the deaf
end shrugs
off the line.

And one of them stays awake
knowing the other won't.

Daily Cup

Youth pulled off like a bandage.
Emotions evaporate a childhood
drift as morning mists
of summer, of mantis and hammock
into the sheer worth of vagueness.

The stale embrace of this home
has become as wanted as
the leftover coffee
cooled by afternoon's exhale.

Uncertainty is welcome
after such repetition of
what is still loved,
what was once loved.

In the understanding
of what differs
between patterns
I always look for newer wounds.
And the coffee warms again.

Slowly lift the cup,
my trembling cascades
summer's own end,
our baptism backwards.

What I taste is bitter,
but what I taste is warm.

Everything Sets

Crawling up
against coffee,
a bed mate who swells,
rolls in pollen a
breathed plume of
awaking fern.

Suns and moons,
the same trees
borrowing shapes of
whalebone
bleaching their reach beneath
a web of stars forgotten
by all who still dream
between this equinox.

This reaction is often
brisk as twitch, ambitious
as cloudshape, any
myth's hesitation.

In the curling steamrise
of breath, I can almost
remember feeling awake,
everything rising and
falling outside.

Backyards

My father always wanted birds,
wet police flares.
He wanted the cold rain
smell stepping on snails,
the soft birth crunch.

But now I hate deciding
what to do with a bookmark
after the last page.

I feel so alike to ending
that I can no longer
fit into my own emptiness.

There were always
too many bottles of
music between us.
There was never a safe step.

I cannot pull wings, and
all sons must become avian.
I could cliché my father
into Daedalus
or say that
injury builds in candle wax,

but silence is well-
worn by us all. In feathers,
the chitin coils of memory
have softened spinal cord
into a single tongue,
speaking heavy words in the clarity
only in backyards.

Wounds

Injury has written claim
in candlewax.

The time swallowing us
whole silences yearn
for betterment with
a complacent sanity,
personifying in hush
unseen scar tissue.

A wound is all
I have left to show
for being wounded.
Healing and forgetting
burn down the same wick.
Our scars don't reminisce enough.

And I have wounds
I never want to fully heal.

Injuries to illustrate
what we've endured,
conquered. Wounds
we flaunt as a trophy
wife or rare illness
for all who care to look.

Age pushes down the monument
of our wounds like a needle.

Time will half
heal the wounded,

but we are not
always grateful
for good reason.

Pyxis

I open the shells of feeling
        into a box.

I had named music
but (in all salt pinches
   and genuine honesties)
wasn't.

In silence
these feelings cocooned
 butterflies sprouted
mariposa parasites of a
pure oxygen blank

pouring out the sky
 with eucalyptus wings.
       Unhanging curtains
       spit sunlight
       in blots of shade.

And the box became music
    vast throbbing harmonies
    dust melodic crescendos,
full-boned hopes
 in each pull of the wings
feeling indistinguishable
from the vacancy of opening.

I have known no other
instrument than the box.

Vanvas

The indifference of innocence
wanders through static
self-destruction as the opposite
of stubborn wandering
rolls in the pollen
of evaporation, steeps
it in staircase.
Exhales family.

Grandfather bloodclot eyes
  peer through layers of glass
  like disembodied cats
  in a petstore.

The haven we have folded you
like a letter yearns
for thick breath,
for a drag of tongue
lies choked with the foreign
atlas of language, dark as
winter's woodsmoke, the mad
burn of innocence.

But we are welcome
here in hollow fruit
egged ambitious, full
of hope in the lack of ritual.
Spontaneity and consistency are
patterns.

But the wet spots of rust,
dimpling organic truth
 hang their age hard

headed and unchanging
as hammock in summer.

Truth is only bitter,
is cold coffee full of grounds
expressed in the indifference
of our innocence
and the innocence of our indifference.

For curiosity
henceforth shall be named want.

And innocence the currency
to be spent blindly for vision
shall leave only indifference,
empty as ice.

Freudenschade

Theravada meditation sleeps
        in the
         ground with
         nirvana-hungry grubs
         chewing on the roots
      of family tree
         tobacco.

Pale-
 fingers grasping
   explain at their onion flesh.
  We can only crawl upwards
roast in sun,

regretting that illumination
        wasn't worth the effort.

Lights can cut   color,
       every sprinkler weeps
       in patterns.

For weeping-in and of itself-wept.
 Deepened
 in the ground, spit hard.
Crawling motioned-
fertilized disappointment.
The rock salt is sewn
with our own eye's hands
   into fresher seas than
those previously sailed
                    upon.

(They lie uncharted,
therefore lifeless.)

Our dead seas
are full of
anchoring scrolls.

Salao

When the city has lost
a day's buoyancy
sinks honey into dusk.
The streets line neighbor
hoods in icewater and marbles.
All of our steps
slack into slips.

Caffeine cracks open
tonight after tonight
like a smile. Let pieces of
moon stay tangled in you
for days. Today, starblood
bleeds the astroveins,
dries awake the galactic morning,
shakes sand out of the towels.
Our oceans realize they
are still instruments, our
landscapes dream, flip coins.

Surface first the mania
howling up water dripping,
submerge cities tangible
enough for sensation.

Let afternoon fall
between the sleeps,
and enough time
gains such face so that
nothing is buoyant, and
leaves no depth to sink.

Doppelgänger
or Spiegel

The eyes of my idolized self
blink its Morse code
as if to wet the soul of footprints.

There is a beat just beneath
the skin. A heart your finger mirrors.
A tap against my chest from both sides.

The blinks take a rhythm
my heart can't encrypt.
Upon the fabric
is burden's sweat
tracing the faces of others.
Faces of hungers.

What has happened has already
happened once,
                sets like sun,
                ages like word.

Their faces left creases
in my recollection,
and I can no longer
name them. I cannot hold
another violin.

The names spell silence
music without.

The eyes of my idolized self
close often, wondering what
of it all will end well.

One Man's Reach

Weave not from the wants,
he tells me,
this is the manifesto
of the wanted.

Asceticism is light
to fascinate the length
of his own shadow.

An allure reverberating
our wineglass stacked culture.
Ruin spit into a napkin.

Some light, he says,
loses the justification
of being mirrored.

Sometimes he laughs.

The Theory of Jar

Bust the method like a mirror,
read the empty until self is
cracked as laughter.

Forget theories,
remember
 embrace salience as you wake
sand through fingertips.

What sticks here is true enough.
Ask anyone. Practice the ask.
Practice everything always.

Confusion can only fill
what was empty. Pretend
intellectualism only as
a quick erase

a comfort burn.
Understanding is a crown
only if collarbone can be too.

Empathy is a bed sheet.
Empathy is an ice cube.
Both of your hands are warm.

On the mirror your palm
left a branched hand of fog.
And for a moment, each finger
breathed thick as laughter.

All Bridges

Those countries we've memorized
comatose mining daylight ore.
Cartographers of this
very heavy couch bridging
the blanks between my sleep.

The caffeine contains a burnt
offering and all of our gods
are decaying in stimulant pools.

Happiness is bridging
blanks between my futures
awakening the couch's lounging gods.

There are dreams drawn
in my head where I am
happier than I am.

How to Break Anything

Notice the dense red
diesel squeeze of anger.
Neck artery metronome, a poetry
for fluffing the pillows
on a deathbed, a poetry
blowing a condom full of air.

I do each,
carefully, in front of you.
So miniscule the tremble
is colored in tenor, skin-
tended wrong tenses for the order

of all the words
that well and bucket.
I could never write the sentence
of walking near enough, or
of cutting the distance
between mouths, but
there's not much any
one can do about that is there?

Be Reaved

I regret my human sleeve
sometimes, sharpening
ingots and ores of now,

(minutes, hours and
  decades to seconds
  hammered together
  molten our age)

  These times
  are not the
  times for regret.

Our world is too
round for a clock to
mean much other
than a tempo, a
meter in a poem or a
beat in the heart,

a song in the mouth,
mute as a jaw of
chewed mirrors.

Smiling throughout
the sometimes you have
used in your studies of self,
you scholarly tooth.

Every age coughs up
characters just like us,

hoping that language will not fail,
but word soft-breaks easy
as skin, and now,

now failure's forged into
something red with uncertain
warmth, something uncaring
and coiled like coldworms
hiding from sunrise.

Sprawling out an ocean
into places cyclical.
Ambitious the way
one looks at a wrist
watch or wrinkle.

Now is our age of failure.
Present flesh rusts
a simple language
to your tongue.
You cannot stay silent.

Lengua Materna

Howl your self back
to the first mouth,
umbilical cut tongue.

Build me a belly
of screams.
Cover my mouth
with one of your
hands.

The Last Wall

Fruits our labor
forgot peel apart
over ripening minutes.

The pieces of things we used
 to love clump
together into new constructions
towering spires-through clouds
                    like hair buds,
clustered and engraved with
 moments.

And now our
memory borrows an alphabet, writes
of needles poking soft into
veiny blue cloudmilk skins
clutched tight
as inhuman attachment, as paradox.
We designed our impermanence

together at a bus stop.
The jealousy here is creation
hidden sparks
roots spurned to bark
aloud with grief.

We wait for the next one,
collect pollen unconnected
to creation, pay in quarters,
pressed to us as health
attached for our own
ripening blink, our wait
for tongue enclosed mouth.

A light in a window
colors something inside.
Behind the fruity glass skin of
the still cooling know
(newborn curtain falls)
stuck in amber,
tree sap whispers begin on through.

Until the light at once dies
                quick as sidewalk
leaving pale crystalline skin
between us-to poke
  with the fingers
  of our children.

Coda

"Table for two,"
one of them would say.

But he came late.
She brought a book.

He wondered how many words she'd read.
And she wondered how many were left.

She broke his ambitions,
and slid them under his door.

He pretended not
to hear her knock.

Breathing Room

Necessity has remained more
alive for longer than art.
Neither spending
enough on the concept alone.

Everything else is
crowning the distraction
and should be mutinied
accordingly in the recycle,
the box that wasn't music
but can try again.

The concept is little
different than water
well frozen over
with concrete
pretend end
to eyelid

There is no language
between us. We have
given enough space
for company, not
enough for one.

Idea Afterbirth

Show me someone
 who can exhale you
entirely with
clean lungs.

Whose end
in itself
 leaves out the pain
 of beginning to burn.

Convince me that
  you didn't mean
   to leave
behind an echo.

What lingers
lies dreaming
of curiosities, oddities
  to fallen family trees.

I'll be coughing
   up afterbirth
  until the blood returns
to take back all this ink.

His Lonely War

There's a feeling to be felt after
a whole day of lying
in bed and
stretching self into my own skin so
tightly the seams pop into fissure
dancing like buttons on glass,
lovers on page.

And the whole night spent
sewing every-
other back together.

Chambers

I cannot keep
rewriting the i
capitalizing my
every isolation.

I am tired of every
thing that fills
the I, the same eye, the
CORRIGAN JAMES MORAN,

this human semi colon,
 hand written
 sloppy youth
  letters like new teeth.
I am living

a run
on sentence.
Everything I have started
is forever beginning.
I am binging in a species
developed too quickly.

My brain is slathered
  with scoops of useless
  processing.

Every cup I've ever held is over
 filling. I can't keep saying
  bitter. I can't keep saying
  cold. I cannot keep rewriting
the question

Why should I only
  have one beginning?

My life's a stanza
  I've force fed full of eraser
  dust, but this map's lined in ink,
  folded in fourths
  for each chamber.

I go for ending
  writing the first word
  of a last sentence, the
  last character of my age.
  I scrape this brain away
  in heavied nights.

In thirsts and smoke
  cold pill tongue hungers
  backed into the brain
  like bones I never broke.

I am binging on endings.
I am becoming a shallow sentence.
I want stanzas of the amygdala.
I want to write lizard brain poetry.

Poems like
  This day started when
  the sleep stopped
  and slowed. I ate an egg.
  This day I am cut into,
  omnivore is the dark grey of rain.
  I will sleep tonight.

Poetry of patient daylights,
unsuffered fitting shapes
of older thought, familiar
breathing. I keep filling
the bottles between us.

I am tired of my definition
of feeling. I am the empty
cold left from boiling.
My ends shivering begin.
Promises, punctuation.

I do not know how
to introduce ending
to you without
changing what we
cannot begin.

If this laughter is our living,
  then death is a dollar menu.
Death is the café crayons.
Death is the door of socks.
  wisdom of heavier
  words somewhere.
Your hand has lost its ink,
hollow for my words to echo
your fearful acoustics.

And now I want lovers to taste
  the dust in my mouth
  from books I'll forget
  once I remember to
  read them,

to taste what I've been trying
  to spit out,
  to taste all these stanzas
  I cannot write down.

But I am only building.
Amygdala is a staircase.

I want my ends like question marks.
I want to know I can write
  ends worth binging,
  an end worth beginning.
I want you to know there is an end.

NGOKO

"For each age is a dream that is dying
Or one that is coming to birth."

-ARTHUR O'SHAUGHNESSY
"Ode"

A Consensual Collapse

You can only sleep in the shape
of the animals that you kill.

As you count your blessings
backwards your skin sweats
  condensation freezing into shape
  of clouds our hungriest
  animal cracker feelings.

The vast dry
  between your teeth
is writing down a question
in counterfeit ink,
asking the difference between
        helping hands and
        umbilical cords.

But your mother tongues
  cut easy as noose, robbing
  unexcused presence in spots
    still unrefined beaten soil
    molten and wounded in garden
      genocides, small town meditations.

With the shape of constitution
and being shaped into
shapeless decay.

This is my plea.

Eulogize yourself in numbers
  and count it backwards
  to find the blessing.

Tell the animals you love
  them with a petri dish.

File your taxes in poetry.

Dig a shapeless hole,
  and plant dreams
  in a garden of cement.

Meditate with the rock
  as your mother asked
  to make your bed.

Because now is the age of sleep,
  old friend. The shape
  of dream is drawn for us, and
I have only slept in the shape
  of the animals I have killed.

Vertebral Column

Heave upon my back all
of yesterday's unknowings,
straighten yourself for
insertion into a lifetime of todays.

Shrug
the implications, consequences,
whatever paves our memory
for ever-increasing yesterdays.

Stir
my coffee with your index finger.
Start
the lawn mower on the first
pull, breathe beauty from heavy
lungs, floss your heart.

Heave,
heave upon my back all
of yesterday's unknowing.
We need
strength for the calendar noose
tug of war
and all of our shoulders have slouched
burnt in rope birth,
fingers bent each from our palm.

Calendar

For
the
men
who
were
months
made
of
hour
glass
jaw
breakers
sucking
their
teeth
and
twirling
their
little
hand
big
hand
tongues.

All of
this was
for you.

A Quiet Momentum

Decades breathed
  into and out
      of no
  one's lungs.

Mincing moon
  meat in salt
  cleaved wet
with motion.

A dry, leafy husk
  lay hanged where
the soul
   once dreamt.

    And I can hold
  an age
 in my hands
 that has never
held youth.

Grandmothers

Jammed sitting in the memories
of my grandparents' house, I
write their smiles yellow bent,
carved drying into paper. I know
I have everything to look
forward to from here.

Because the butterfly nets that once
held our past inside like an hour
glass have grown sponge-holes
mouths meant for nothing.
Dry swallowing memory.
Dry heaves.

The brain of our grand
father has been eaten by God's
own antfarm. Slicking
oil to shower tile,
waiting for the slip.

The binds that once held
our memory
have become shackles, sorrows, an
ease of certainty
cutting with distance.

Lost upon no known sea
the sirens who were once
our daughters scream in the
languages of rotting meat.

Look back
towards shore.

For once the butterfly nets have grown
their holes, these
colors no longer stay.

Separation Anxiety

She colors through sand her movement,
and not the colors of the
impressionists or manskin,
but the shades of senses
dreaming a subtle palm of sleep.

And she moves gracefully
plucking the air of August
　from god's only lung
　to be carried like a bottle.

For this,
she bears a mark of burden
shaped in sundial,
　tracing the same shadow through
　different days

a
　quiet
　　momentum

My bones have broken their backs
　trying to slow
　her progress.

My angels have pulled out their wings
and borrowed my legs.
The feathers they stuck with fists into
the trees
to feel their way back after she
has drunken the color to a yawn.

The angels sing each
ending backwards
during morning meditation.
Their voices the fall of unclimbed
trees, counting solemnly
on their fingers the empires
she moves through.
The vast-throbbed harmonies
and webbing crescendos of dust
her rainmaking bones.

The pop-out children's books of
heaven have turned to glass.

The voices of my following
follow through sand with mouth
only blooded. Full and wet
with resonant teeth.

I can say now
she has counted her love in footprints.
From this distance
neither of us is to be trusted.

Fake War Story

There was a
  time when I forgot how
  to zip
up a stomach.

There were days during
which I remembered
 mathematics before numbers
 and sorrow before the tongue.

There are futures I
long to know
whereby all other
realizations lie

as silent
as the grubs beneath our feet,
knowing us full only
by the prose of our footfalls.

Cooking in the Hot
Tub of Immortality

I have learned that this
  was not some
  thing, this want
  for unquiet to ripple
across silent surfaces,

this scratch for your words
  smoothing veins through
  soil, shallow depths
  dust to earth nostalgic.

Want cannot be divided
in the spread of roots.

Want spends ancient time
  tables and firmament
  sails to work itself
  over the unrecalling rocks
  feeling Atlas's shoulders
  gnash under ennui.

Joystrung to an esophagus,
  warmed by
  two lungs

tickling the winds
  who likewise react—
  sucked in, this
  feathery hubris.

And the envelope
  evaporated the taste

of what held it together,
  the charred ecstatic
  machinery of new beauty.

Upon the first of ice, a
  child's tongue wheel
  barrow dragged, a face
  recalled during holiday dinners,
  smiles greasing every
  one you loved.

Ripples fascinate
  stuck with your sun
  dew to bare skin.
  A new skin, but
  you remain

forgotten in the shape
  of boredom's enamor.
  Instinct's enamel.

The pieces of me
  boil our selves
  further into these
  cocooning stanzas.

Age is an echo
  full of us waiting
  to react
  to something beginning.

Burnt Offering

Our eyes four
glasses of glinting
flint, meeting their
laughterous heats.

Something sure
to burn, my heart
of beating ashes.

The iced click
of a locked door,
ember kindling distance
until our eyes crashed.

Nothing is Late

All of my lovers are over
due library books.

There is a map
to the creases
you left.

The pages of books dog-
eared, future in a fold.
There's an end to the
endlessness in it.

There is beauty
in burning poems without
heat, and loving without
noticing if overdue.

I turn every
one I love
into librarians.

I wish I could believe
there is nothing
beautiful in that.

Enrich Ending

I am nothing that you are not.
My words have been
weighted in smoke,
these lungs softened
by morning. Nothing
I say can change
what I cannot.

She is endless in a
cough, in a wall of
uncharted stars, hair
puddling rainwater.
Happiness in an hour
and a half.
Laughter spread over an age.

I can say with certainty's own unease,
I have written the only line I will be
remembered for.
She is worth her wait in war.

Those Bright Windows

From where you can see
I am a whiff of hunger
in a handful of bakers.

The light tonguing out
night breathing nowhere in.
Lunar dough full of hands
kneading.

Peopled shapes separated by glass,
folded in fourths, epigraph framed,
each hungering some
dowsed equal glow
the shapes of people like shoelaces.

And here I remain on neither
side of the window, this
drowsy scent of want.

The Most Important
Moment in a Life

And here we are entirely
tenth graded into this moment.

Standing still now is sipping
 a cup of room temperature milk.

 Our lips take to the color
 of young bone, the color
 of sun just behind some
 shapeless cloud.

Reasons

My life has been forgotten
  by the world's longest pencil.

The every of once
    wraps itself to the fibers
    in corndog sticks and
    crucifixes.

In the chance
   of identical dreams
 our silent movie ears
all hear the same plea.

And that is
    do not react.

Reaction is continuation
  continuation is delay
  to delay is to wither
  withering is aging
  and through age comes
  some meaningless end.

Reaction is the only poetry
  worth shackling to sentence.

This is a letter from the end
of nothing in particular.
Yours truly.

From here,
we can move no further in any

direction than where we have been.
There is a reason we are circular.

Our fragility is reread
and worn down to notice
every door
opened will close behind you.

Soon you will react,
        flip this page,
and everything will be different.

You're getting closer to the end,
  but there really
  is no other way.

The First Wall

You've hidden the same truth
in different lies.

Being stuck with permanence
and feeling an opposite
tremble towards a
baptism you cannot
remember.

One is counting bandages
and the other is
counting wounds.

Jisei

Writing up words
 while tar ink bubbles
on the disappointed end of
twisted smoke.

The world is god's chronogram,
our memoir, and each lick
of the anvil, each flip of
a page, an age brings about
the end.

Call it a scavenger hunt.
Find the personalities
that only fit in ash.
Begin to read.

An Almost Rusted Cage

The reason I have walked
 in different directions
  is some primal relic
   of a being I no longer am in
    full.

     Our renovated apartment
    lost in dry cleaning,
   deepening holes dug by a stranger
  of similar descent, all around.

Shoveling neurons into this same
  hole
    clutched together
   these unborn twins, hands
 full of seeds tossed in
abstract painting.

Tightens the throat
    in the kind of fear
    that waxes the wings
    of inconsistency.

Mudita

I sit upon mushroom petals,
   pouring myself into
too many empty cups.
Perhaps waiting
    to be discovered
    as something less than I let on.

Waiting to the echoes
    of crickets taking
the edges of light,
but you alone know
    the shape of my dreams.

In my awkward stretch through
  this world I have come to
    gift diseasing kings, crowns
     and crayons while
    I wait outside
    for the wrong person.

A growth inside with
the lukewarm lemonade
feel telling me
there's never really a right
person to wait for, never a
beginning planned to end.

And the moths in the stomach
    care not for caterpillars
    as this truth
    gnawed free, screams.

Undecided between the beauty
            and the fear
            of the thought undone,
I rest beginning as I must rest my end.

Silence composes its insects
    under an overcast dilemma.
    Name me a sky

under which I remain
waiting for a reason to wait.

But the clockwork doesn't stop
        cogs moving to rust,
        but even that feels wrong.
         Grandparents skin their
        chameleoned
         christmas card ambition, but I
         only miss the hands folding them.
     And the principle of my feeling
    accepts the necessity as it
 steeps, tealeafed and tip
toeing into animal shape.

How I envy their whole
    splendor and fear
    bitterness and salve
    the word and the teeth
    innocence and indifference
    powdered to throats
    forgotten, powerful as burn
    to taste soft as butterfly net.

My envy has diluted
all I could make into music.
 The songs to save left
  unsung as wet matches.

Confused without discovery only the
striking without the warmth.
I am sitting.
I am waiting.
I have dreamt only
to hide the sleep.

Teeth

I have dripped out
the wake
          (in tune with a slow
   heartbeat
              a finger tipping against my
   skin)
     right as blood's unbeaten
hearts of places no one
has stepped upon in the right
pair of shoes.

The canvassed flesh color
        of filled holes
under hot, colorless suns,
   my sons have grown vague, round
   and gaunt as gravity
   tugging their descent,
   their angelwing membrane.

The indecision between their
   bones is only innocence, a dream
   between us, hourglass of
   wine and ice of simple lust.

There are others falling too,
he tells me,
that nothing ever really ends.

He echoes back into the closed envelope
the bitter cup where
someone else's children will steep.
Each hunger of our smiles mapped
whole countries with our sleep.

The children's books of heaven
have always been atlases.
And now each harbors the opposite
crave in frowned eyes
day dreaming in
between us
an ojo.

There isn't a single truth
left to our bones. Only
the cutsmiled holes of memory.
Only the blind
kingdoms of ancestry,
neon exonyms, the madness of
limiting everyone's madness.

What holds me here will go
away
through an egg

shell to skin,
the sewn selves of my blood
line up like stanzas
like firing squad.

Our edges seem gentle
as metaphor. The teeth
truly hidden with word.

A Bored Man
Walks through Ostia

There are street light
shutters on the eyes
of my head, only showing
the stops, the yields,
and the gos at angles.
Characters are always
nearing,

and the man who
knows how to help me
is carrying a hand
full of candle wax
ribboning down his palm.

Drying quicker than he can
realize, the ice cubes in
his glass are practicing the
opposite. His existence
is letters away
from a palindrome.

My stagnation is quoting
itself into redundancy.
All I want is for the return
angle closing, illuminating
inner want. This want separate
from the angle, free from
understanding.
This salvation without angels.
This damnation without angels.

My existence fits in a teabag.
I was born waiting to boil.
Every cup that's ever held
me is overfilling. He has
tasted what I am to become.
I can only watch him go.

Nature Rolling off
the Human Tongue

In the spans of
nothing is nothing
natural is the blink,
blessed is the blink,
and the tickling in our instinct
(the cold hair of our veinthought
      fists pulling out at the roots)
tickles even the ticklish-
                  -ticking as the
            clock's beat of a hearty
                              lunchtime.
Keeps the star charts fat,
    (stretch-marked constellations)
    making the above
            only true
            and
            only truer.

The teeth lying
behind the tongue
of our every surreal communion-
          in the name of the father,
      digesting damnation to
rule over the slow muscular
                        gallops in
                        to and after
            that single
birth we all share,

this easiest kind of salvation.

Oh
this lie bloats our shape
        as the moon wanes
                and swells,
but covers stars like an eye-patch
rolling a lie
off the tongue true.

With Our Mirth

Empires are beaten
off to a ball of the thumb.
The globes of blood drawn
by dynasty lick
the orbit of sin
but always wish for the
taste of sinner.

Blind kings
throw rocks
in no real direction at all.

Batik

A heart can be cut
in eight ways before
coming to resemble
a landscape.

Cardiacs must fear the beauty of
brokenness, the snowglobing net
of language inadequate.
Brokenness captures
all of entirety's potential
in a juvenile mouthful.

The lucky ones are born whole.
Time and effort interrupt the self,
splintering the pages of us glass
atlases,
folding the map into creases.

A compass can be shaken in
any direction before
our cartography succumbs
to character.

Flip through the atlases of
pointlessness. These hearts
are always easier to split
into pieces. Look instead
for the creases, drag
from your tongue
the latitude of age to
the longitude of your hunger,
and pull.

We will each find
our landscapes of nothing,
splitting apart pages.

Earth Tongues

All of my friends were immortal
before me. These are those
who say time is not
on our dancing shoes.

These boys with coffee cups
and big pupils holding
the smoke in.

These boys with maggot skin,
slinging their bodies
heavy and dripping
with another soul.

I was boiling before
their pens, before
these characters
were hungry for
what they could
chew from our age.
What they left
is this hunger no
page can repress.

Makers all become monsters.

Characters of Age

I know them well enough to say
they stick not to one age.

Each of their fingers beats a new dent
into your heart,
screams some stanza of untied shoes.
Messages they write into mirrors
I've hidden in the ash
a pillar of pleas.

Our shamans have given us gifts
of vision, of curiosity, rock and want.
Of broken mirrors and loose jaws, blood
spitting angel flaps.

The children's books of heaven
had too few pages all along.
Against broken glass
our bones suck themselves full
again with the marrow of youth.

We taste of sinner at last
our cup is warm, bitter. All
four chambers beating
full and wet.

The characters leach their essence
steeping into the ages, their
untasted loves
baptize in reverse.

In the wait,
I have been forgotten.

By whom, he says,
I have killed for
our sleep, for our
shape of dream.

The animals now hide
behind teeth of my words,
  they have sewn spiderwebs in my hair.

The momentum of ending
now rings in prose, falls from stanza
to slug in song
to hold in box
in bookshelves, in rust.
In heaven, in here.
In a home, now
afternoon.

The wristwatch has creased the wrinkle,
the age is only wait.
Patterns choruses.
Choiceless

the sea has learned
to swallow the sun.

Each day
eases your mark of burden
from the pen of my reach.

For this,
you have eaten me whole,
kicked the hourglass,

fogged the mirror with your hand,
opening your porous maw
that day you turned and drove to work
evaporating. You
are reaction. You
have been all along.

I am a want for unchange,
for steeping, for timelines
mattering for the sip.

I am one of many inhaled
and exhaled by days.
These lungs are boxes that will
never really close.
These chambers had nothing to
do with my heart.

Forgotten and reminisced, I tell him,
I tell my self
there is a cycle here,
just beneath the skin.

This cannot be broken
easy as bone.

What We Are

I once misread a sentence
from a piece my sister painted
that read
WE ARE NOTHING
BUT LOVELY BUFFETS OF ENERGY

And she corrected me with
BUFFETS really reading as BURSTS,
both having their opposite's
charm. As all the music I've loved is
soaked in an ocean of forgotten clicks
library's full of card
boarded human experience.

This music jumbled together with
the paintings and pocket novels.
We are making our selves into buffets
by basking in buffets.
Binging in art
mineraled water
note padded, no nose breathing.

All I have
read
boils down to everything
I have read.

Nothing happens in bursts.
I find nobody beyond boiling,
none who have not steeped.

Art is seventy-five
percent of the human body.
Blessed is the binge.

Art is all close
to water in our mouths,
stomach's tilled
with whiskers.
Buffets really reading as buffets.

You Know How it Begins

With little burns
 in old films,
time capsules
  land mined
  into the dirt.

Lit sparsely
 with brittle sands,
reflected off the watch's glass
 a sleeping star
cold as bedlamp-
 broken fingers
pointing at the destination.

Through fingertip, the
regret of reflection forms soft
stabs old holes
 into the set potentials of happiness.
Moves no destination, but stretches
    far too thin the time before it.

And this conflict glows into
notice by
  way of combustion
burning to butterfly sprigs
    of rosemary veins
and oleander arteries
all composing the smell
        of faded beauty.

That fond smell
   thickened in mistflesh
that hides the burns.

The same drowned star waiting
to drip its ocean free
burns premonition into a single point
and from here, you know how it ends.

Foil

First,
love falls into a buttoned collar
bone splinters its sex grenade
winestain washes determined
memory, cares less, forgets.

Outer,
soil smells no different
in shovel the bodies were just tulips,
bounced eggs-strung spaghetti
weaves basket case our asylum.

Inner,
the core is harder
to adapt, here are the seeds
in a counselor's couch high-
jacked plane cock pit
fight to produce right angle
stops yields goes.

Last,
romance novel closes into jaw
line for junkyard sprinkled
cut as long wrists or
taxes to bring about the only
marks of our sole equation.

Solution undefined,
repeating.

A Serious Question

In this moment you are busy
with your forefathers porking
your foremothers in hanging
gardens of soymilk.

The bacon of their lovemaking
transcends the poppy
children ancestry, timelines
plating tea, a soft music.

They have spent their steeps,
their free refills pouring
you warm
into the cup of now, but you
are not the cup.
You cannot be tasted
nor taste because you are
tastebuds and the time
lines matter as much as
coke lines or waiting lines.

So razor
blade the breath and breathe
it in.

Soon you'll pour your own age,
evaporate like a wet dream.
Our descent is printed with
an expiration date, curves
to the lowest point, asymptotic
offspring. How creation ends
without question. The answer
earlier in the sentence.

Salve

Sublime films upon one's skin
 (where the bandage took sweat)
  hearing the stale tenderness
  within the calming
  words, gnarled and rasp
  blooming
  in the meat-lockered
  means of gluing wombs
  to the inside.

The process is familiar
   as well-known tendencies
   in response to people you
 love
 living

too slowly for
 seas to carry all
   delicacy of youth

too lovely for
  us to damn with the
     anchor of poetry.

But as the tenderness sets
 into the flesh of
   one's intellect
we all try our
   luck and spin roulettes
we can no longer see.

The more it's seen
   it becomes obvious

that what blooms as human
withers
withers to nothing at all.

Upon No Known Sea

The way the spoon
    creaks
beneath the sun
  mouthed by butane by flame.

Pulling fumes
 through the methpipe
of someone else's opinion.

Smiled shards melt from
  the roundness of our moon
 into the lunar playdough
cut to pieces by toenails
    of obsidian and
the own eye's pupil
    peeled a dilation dark from
razorblade.

She mentions the eyes
 first, but
        it delves
          sideways
        like a sailor

  working medicine
  into mutiny,
 tracing stretchmarks
in his listening.

He licks wind into sail
threaded with strands of hair
 once grown
  from someone

loved so much,
but now neither can remember why.

Ambitiously Empty

I often mistake you
for the empty space in
between people sitting on a bench.

KRAMANTARA

Atlas

After waking up with you I left
some dream
steeping the opaque high
in our shivering vision that
pondered us down
back enough
to feel what we once felt
was enough.

Dragging my mouth up
you and leaving a
wet lexicon upon
your kneecaps.
This map of you
folding into me.

What I am doing
is tangling our depths,
tying anchor veins to these fingertips
we're tracing over each
other, giving names to
densities of flesh
in place of memory.

These pieces of us,
wind chimes breathing
every tree from the
forts full of sun,
from our love
of empty forests.
Our tongueless gusts
drying where your
mouth rose from me,

where my back
has been carved
in every history
every name we
shared.

The red letters
falling to
the color of skin
scraped lean just
above blood.

Each letter fallen
a dark field of candles
balancing my spine.
Aloud a sentenced
syllable of roses
fluffing open their
morning hold
of us beside our
limbed tangling,
our red bones connected.
In cartilage dreaming.

And in this
sleep beneath us,
we'll leave
pulled up bruises
on each other
to the neck,
our bodies weaving
together their
tangled veins.
You and I

taking two petals
off with our teeth.
close me with them
into your pages.
Trim the living
world to leave it wet
in vases between us,
speak your mouth against
my neck, suck up this bruising
language of making me yours.
Keep my dead world mapped
against your chest.

Your fingernails into
my back, the weight
of these roses
taking a deep breath.

Coughing across
your thighs,
skytopped where waves
full of salt touched clouds
over countries half unread,
forested pages we closed only to
flatten flowers we'd find later.

The taste of you here
the atlas of us shadowing
this together sun. You

beneath a simple layer
lust out the edges of mouth.
Your fist heavy with my hair.
So this candle such
wheels our spoken
hands together,

while the end
waits a glass of
water beside your bed.

That much is missed
beneath the measured
mangling of our ends,
our gulping together.

Our mapping of each
other's dreams. Always
measuring the distance
between small flames.
Asking you in those
morning blankets
to cross my heart
in your early tongue,

to speak to me
in your words that
only held wind
chimed warmth,
pushing together
what is beneath our bodies.

Reverse my childhood
through your angle
of daylight. With you
I can name each of
our knots like different winds.
I want to know our distance
from every dream
we forgot before waking.